THE
BASIC
GRAMMAR

© *Robert Gibson & Sons, Glasgow, Limited, 1987*

ISBN 0 7169 4075 2

ROBERT GIBSON & SONS, GLASGOW, LTD.
17 Fitzroy Place, Glasgow, G3 7SF, Scotland, U.K.

FOREWORD

THIS LITTLE GRAMMAR has been written specially for the requirements of pupils and its aim is to lead them from the earliest stages. The writer has therefore endeavoured to render the subject as simple and as clear as possible.

Perhaps the amount of Grammar learned is not of so much importance as the manner of learning. From the very first the pupils ought to be trained to think in a scientific way. In learning the Parts of Speech, the function of the words must be determined first, and then, in consequence of that function, the name of the Part of Speech given.

For example, the pupils should not be told anything about a Noun, but asked to pick out from a selected passage all the names of things before they are told what a noun is. All other Parts of Speech should be dealt with in the same way, the procedure being always from the function to the name.

In dealing with Analysis, the writer has introduced the term Nominative to avoid confusion of thought as to what is the subject — a phrase or a word. It has the further advantage of preparing the way for the teaching of Case.

CONTENTS

PART I

PART II

3

PART I

NOUNS

Read:

Down dived the frogman into the deep water, and brought up the child. The brave frogman laid the child on the grass, and the mother with a joyful cry picked up the child.

Pick out all the words that are names of things:

Frogman, water, child, frogman, child, grass, mother, cry, child.

These words are the NAMES of something, and we call them NOUNS, for noun means name.

A NOUN is the name of any person, place, animal or thing.

A NOUN is a NAMING WORD.

EXERCISE 1

(a) *Pick out the Nouns in the following sentences:*
1. Birds eat worms.
2. Robert burnt his fingers.
3. The girl reads stories.
4. Spiders weave webs.
5. The hens have laid some fine eggs.
6. The sun rises in the morning and sets in the evening.
7. The porters in the warehouse carry heavy loads.
8. The butcher had a row of sausages in the window.
9. In the meadow the lambs were playing round their mothers.
10. The croaking frog leapt quickly into the water.

(b) *Pick out Nouns from suitable sentences in your school Reader.*

VERBS

Read the paragraph about the frogman and pick out all the words that tell us what he did or what the mother did.

These words, dived, brought, laid, picked, which tell us what someone or something did, are called VERBS.

We may now say that **a VERB is a DOING WORD.**

4

Pick out the Verbs in the following sentences:
1. He gave the boy a coin.
2. A little spark kindled a great fire.
3. The girl ran well and won a prize.
4. He goes to church on Sunday.
5. An old tree grew near the garden gate.
6. She wandered up and down.
7. The minister spoke a few words.
8. The summer sun shone brightly.
9. The king sat on his royal throne.
10. Tonight no moon we see.
11. Come and sit under this tree.
12. A pleasanter spot you never spied.
13. Run away and play.
14. The gardeners dug a deep trench.
15. The horse came when I whistled.

EXERCISE 3

Make sentences using the following Verbs:
(a) Go, sit, runs, chase, throws, plays, win, think, says, walks, come, writes, builds, fight, cross, sail.
(b) Arrived, dug, came, swam, sang, drove, saw, flew, marched, ate, told, taught, learned, heard, went.

There are only a few verbs which may not be looked upon as *doing words*, and they should be committed to memory.

These verbs are known as *auxiliary* or *helping* verbs. They help another verb to form a complete tense, e.g. He has gone, I shall sing, I might go.

The following is a list:

Am, is, are, was, were, be, being, been, have, has, had, shall, should, will, would, can, could, may, might, must.

EXERCISE 4

(a) *Make sentences, using the aforementioned Verbs.*
(b) *Pick out Verbs from suitable sentences in your school Reader.*

PRONOUNS

Read:

> When Robert entered the room, Robert picked up a book. This book belonged to Robert's sister. The book was of no use to Robert's sister, as Robert's sister had read the book already. When Robert's sister was given a book of Robert's to read in exchange, both Robert and Robert's sister were satisfied.

The pupils will probably feel that the paragraph is not good. Ask them to put in suitable words.

The paragraph corrected will then be:

> When Robert entered the room, *he* picked up a book. The book belonged to *his* sister. *It* was of no use to *her*, as *she* had read *it* already. When *she* was given a book of *his* to read in exchange, *they* were both satisfied.

The words, *he, his, it, her, she, they,* are put in place of *nouns*, and because they stand for Nouns they are called PRONOUNS.

A PRONOUN is a word that stands for a Noun.

List of Pronouns:

> I, mine, me, we, ours, us, you, yours, he, his, him, she, hers, her, it, its, they, theirs, them, this, those who, whose, whom, which, that.

EXERCISE 5

Pick out the Pronouns in the following sentences:

1. We do not know where he puts his book.
2. The girl for whom you were looking is here.
3. The new house is ours, the old one is his.
4. Everyone is expected to work hard.
5. I do not know where they have gone.
6. That is the man who built the house.
7. Did you see them on the pier?
8. The atlas is theirs, not yours.
9. Who was the man with you?
10. Those are not my boots.
11. This is my pen. Where did you find it?
12. She says the pen is hers.

6

(a) Make sentences using the Pronouns on page 6.

(b) Pick out Pronouns from sentences in your school Reader.

ADJECTIVES

Read:

Grandma, as the children called her, was old and bent. Her little, one-storied house stood next to the school, and she had a cheerful smile for every boy and girl that passed.

Pick out the words which describe a noun:

Old, bent, little, one-storied, cheerful, every.

These words describe a Noun, and are, therefore, called ADJECTIVES.

An ADJECTIVE is a word which describes or qualifies a Noun or Pronoun.

EXERCISE 7

Pick out Nouns and then the Adjectives that describe them:

1. He was a brave lad.
2. The little boy kept two rabbits.
3. Mary had a pet lamb.
4. Every man was in his proper place.
5. He had much pain.
6. The little girl has some beautiful toys.
7. A half-loaf is better than no bread.
8. The night was dark.
9. The way was long, the wind was cold, the minstrel was infirm and old.

EXERCISE 8

(a) Make sentences using the following Adjectives:

Dark, brave, find, big, seven, old, few, young, large, many, free, thin, grey, brown, clever, kind, idle, guilty, fourth, cold, warm, hot, good, fast, slow, beautiful, several, safe, dangerous, powerful, comfortable.

(b) Pick out Adjectives from sentences in your school Reader.

ADVERBS

Read:

Then Betty quietly opened the door of the cage and allowed Pert to fly out. He hopped about and played merrily with his brothers and sisters.

Pick out all the verbs, and then the words which in some way describe those verbs.

'Then' tells *when* Betty opened, and 'quietly' tells *how* she opened the door. 'Out' tells *where* Pert flew; 'about' tells *how* he hopped, and 'merrily' tells *how* he played.

These words, *then, quietly, out, about, merrily*, are called ADVERBS, because they describe or attach themselves to a Verb.

Adverbs tell HOW, WHEN and WHERE a thing is done and so are called Adverbs of Manner, Time and Place.

Although their chief work is to describe Verbs, ADVERBS describe or modify other parts of speech, as Adjectives and Adverbs.

Examples: The work was *very* hard (modifying adj.).
He ran *so* fast that he escaped (mod. adv.).
She came *quite* near (mod. adv.).
It is *not* fair (mod. adj.).

Note: Not, very, too, so and *quite* are adverbs of degree.

ADJECTIVES DESCRIBE OR QUALIFY NOUNS OR PRONOUNS.

ADVERBS describe or modify any other part of speech, except a NOUN or PRONOUN.

EXERCISE 9

Pick out the Adverbs in the following sentences:

1. The boy came early and stayed late.
2. The captain spoke sharply.
3. The river flows fast.
4. The girl came home yesterday.
5. He was not late.
6. The birds sang sweetly.
7. The father worked very hard.
8. The shepherd heard quite well.
9. Sit still.
10. Slowly and sadly we laid him down.

8

11. The poor man was very grateful.
12. Down there do the dear little flowers lie?
13. He was so tired that he immediately fell asleep.
14. The fiery fight is heard no more.
15. How pleasant the life of a bird must be.
16. The master was very much disappointed.
17. This boy is not as tall as his sister.
18. He was better informed than I was.
19. He is very clever but rather indolent.

EXERCISE 10

(a) *Make sentences using the following Adverbs:*

Badly, silently, down, up, in, quickly, off, wisely, late, early, better, well, comfortably, worse, forward, most, fast, far, much, past, long, enough, distantly, once, sometimes, always, not, along, on, in and out, now and then, backwards and forwards.

(b) *Pick out Adverbs from sentences in your school Reader.*

PREPOSITIONS

The pencil is   in   my hand.
       "   above   "
       "   below   "
       "   beside   "
       "   under   "
       "   over   "

These words, *in, above, below, beside, under, over,* show the relation between *pencil* and *hand.*

We call these words PREPOSITIONS.

A PREPOSITION is a word which shows the relation between a noun or pronoun and some other word in the sentence.

Note: Prepositions form, with a noun, either an adjectival or an adverbial phrase.

        A man *of honour* (adj.).
        The hat *with a blue band* (adj.).
        He entered *with confidence* (adv.).

9

ADVERBS and PREPOSITIONS can be confused. The rule is that a preposition is always 'positioned' before another word, but an adverb stands alone.

He waited outside the house (preposition).
He waited outside (adverb).

EXERCISE 11

Pick out the Prepositions in the following sentences:

1. The desk is in the corner.
2. The map is on the wall.
3. Tom is at the bottom of the class.
4. He walked along the street to the corner.
5. The village lies beyond the river.
6. The horse was taken to the river.
7. A letter came from London on Saturday.
8. He remained with us until Monday morning.
9. He stood in the rain without an umbrella.
10. Opposite the church was a fine statue.
11. Across his brow his hand he drew.
12. At home no fire had he.

EXERCISE 12

(a) *Make sentences using the following Prepositions:*
By, of, upon, behind, before, for, beside, through, into, between, within, during, until, after, against, around, among, near, past, since.

(b) *Pick out Prepositions from sentences in your school Reader.*

ANALYSIS.

SIMPLE SENTENCES

To analyse a sentence is to break it up into its separate parts and to show how those parts are related to one another.

Every sentence is made up of two parts.

 (i) What we speak about.
 (ii) What we say about it.

What we speak about is the SUBJECT.

What we say about the Subject is the PREDICATE.

> Birds fly.

In this sentence we speak about *birds*, and, therefore, 'birds' is the SUBJECT.

We say they *fly*, therefore, 'fly' is the PREDICATE.

The SUBJECT consists of 'NAMING WORDS'.
The PREDICATE consists of 'DOING WORDS'.

SCHEME OF TABULAR ANALYSIS.

SUBJECT	PREDICATE
Birds	fly

Some beautiful birds fly in and out of our barn.

SUBJECT	PREDICATE
Some beautiful birds	fly in and out of our barn

The farmer's son is a very big boy.

SUBJECT	PREDICATE
The farmer's son	is a very big boy

Note: When there are more nouns than one in a sentence, we must be perfectly clear which noun is the subject.

Compare:

(a)   The boy broke the window.

(b)   The window was broken by the boy.

These two sentences tell us the same thing, but in a different way.

In *(a)* we are speaking about the *boy*, not the window.

In *(b)* we are speaking of the *window*, not the boy.

In *(a)* the *boy* is the subject.

In *(b)* the *window* is the subject.

See *Active and Passive Voice* (page 30).

Analyse into Subject and Predicate:

1. Dogs bark.
2. Fish swim.
3. The house was burned.
4. The wall was high.
5. The pony galloped away.
6. The boy broke the window.
7. The window was broken by the boy.
8. We visited the museum.
9. The hay in the field was sold yesterday.
10. The house on the top of the hill belongs to my uncle.
11. The ships took refuge in the harbour.
12. Swimming is a pleasant exercise.
13. To assist the wounded was their duty.
14. What has happened?
15. Which will you take?
16. Where is my hat?
17. Far away from home and friends, the emigrant felt homesick.
18. Yesterday in the field I sold all my hay.
19. Faster and faster sped the horse over the solid ground.
20. Farther and farther spread the pain over his side.
21. Sit still.
22. Then in came Randolph Murray.
23. Through the window long I gazed.
24. The soldiers, mourning their lost leader, filed slowly past.

OBJECT

Analyse: Cats catch mice.

Subject — Cats.   Predicate — Catch mice.

Note here that the *predicate* is made up of two words, a *verb* and a *noun*. The verb 'catch' tells us what the cats do. The action does not remain with the cats, but is directed to the mice. In other words, something is done to the mice. We say, then, that Mice is the OBJECT, or the ACCUSATIVE CASE.

Pick out the Object in the following sentences:
1. The teacher opened the window.
2. He saw a horse.
3. The boy broke the pen.
4. Tom plays football.
5. The girl dressed a doll.
6. She knitted a sock.
7. The fisherman caught a big fish.
8. The warrior bowed his crested head.
9. The shepherds watched their flocks.
10. Little strokes fell great oaks.
11. The wolf devoured the little lamb.
12. James saw them in the town.
13. She delighted us with her songs.
14. His country called him, and he obeyed the call.

Analyse: The watchful cats catch many mice in the old barn.

SUBJECT		PREDICATE		
The watchful cats		catch many mice in the old barn.		
ENLARG. OF NOM.	NOM.	VERB	OBJECT	EXTENSION (OF VERB)
The watchful	cats	catch	many mice	in the old barn. *(place)*

The SUBJECT is made up of two parts.
(i) The Nominative, 'cats', which is the *name* of what we are speaking about.
(ii) The ENLARGEMENT of the Nominative, 'The watchful', which is an adjectival phrase describing 'cats'.

The PREDICATE is divided into three parts:
(i) The Verb 'catch'.
(ii) The Object, 'many mice'.
(iii) The Extension, which is the name given to any adverbial expression modifying the Verb.

13

Analyse on the above plan:

1. We met a little girl this morning.
2. The lark sang merrily in the sky.
3. They all ran after the farmer's wife.
4. She cut off their tails with a carving knife.
5. The boy stood on the burning deck.
6. He goes on Sunday to the church.
7. He hears his daughter's voice.
8. His father's sword he has girded on.
9. A rolling stone gathers no moss.
10. She sweetly sang a beautiful hymn.
11. A hungry bird came daily to my window.
12. Here we suffer grief and pain.
13. Last night the moon had a golden ring.
14. Then an open field they crossed.
15. The spiders from their cobwebs peep.
16. Down ran the wine into the road.
17. The baron's dwarf his courser held.
18. The gallant hound the wolf had slain.
19. Among the hills a wandering life I led.
20. Soft in the breeze the bluebells sigh.

THE COMPLEMENT

Some verbs:

Am, is, are, was, were, be, been, being, appear, seem, become —
require some other part of speech to make the sense complete.

When we say 'London is' we feel something is wanting.

When we say 'London is a great city,' the sense is complete, and we
have a sentence.

The words, 'a great city', which were added to complete the sentence,
are called the COMPLEMENT.

Observe that the complement, when a noun, refers always to the same
thing as the Nominative, and that nothing is done to it. That is to say,
that it suffers no action.

Examples of Complement:

> The boy became *a great poet*.
> Nelson was *a national hero*.
> This boy is *very clever*.
> He is *a splendid swimmer*.
> The house seems *perfectly suitable*.

Analyse: Nairobi has now become a large city.

SUBJECT	PREDICATE		
Nairobi	has now become a large city.		
ENL. OF NOM. NOM.	VERB	COMPLE-MENT	EXTENSION
Nairobi	has become	a large city	now *(time)*

EXERCISE 16

Analyse on the same plan:

1. He was a great man.
2. She seems a very clever girl.
3. You are becoming a good swimmer.
4. These leaves are very beautiful.
5. The summer morn is bright and fair.
6. His life was full of care.
7. A rare old plant is the ivy green.
8. The heath this night must be my bed.
9. Two merry gipsies are we.
10. James was often at the top of his class.
11. A farmer's life's the life for me.
12. In this winter weather cold must be your nest.

15

Complete Scheme of Analysis.

Some boys pulled down the old nests last year.

SUBJECT		PREDICATE			
Some boys		Pulled down the old nests last year.			
ENL. OF NOM.	NOM	VERB	ENL. OF OBJ.	OBJ.	EXTENS-ION
Some	boys	pulled	the old	nests	down *(place)* last year *(time)*

EXERCISE 17

Analyse on the same plan:

1. The ships took refuge in the harbour.
2. In the early morning we went aboard.
3. A stranger with a dog was sitting on the stile.
4. Forty flags with their crimson bars flashed in the morning wind.
5. Through the smoke and flames the fireman pushed his way.
6. You must come in to do your lessons.
7. Always play the game.
8. Into the valley of death rode the six hundred.
9. In after years this boy became a very great man.
10. Through glowing orchards forth they peep.
11. Adown the glen rode armed men.
12. Put on your hat.
13. In her attic window the staff she set.
14. Honour thy father and thy mother.
15. Green grows the grass above the warrior's grave.
16. Beneath each fairy footfall sprang a little flower.
17. She went to the baker's to buy him some bread.
18. Sometimes in winter these strange people find on the shore the wreck of a ship.
19. The poor ye have always with you.
20. What are you doing, you little old man?

21. Where are you going, my pretty maid?
22. Around the fire one wintry night,
    The farmer's rosy children sat.
23. Rest thy weary head upon this breast.
24. They love to catch the burning sparks.
25. A foolish son is a grief to his father.
26. The budding twigs spread out their fan to catch the breezy air.
27. Bruce with the pilot's wary eye, the slackening of the storm could spy.
28. The lazy lad likes to lie under the lime trees.
29. Hast thou a star to guide thy path?
30. Pearly drops of dew we drink
    In acorn cups filled to the brink.

SYNTHESIS

Supply Enlargements of the Nominative.

(a) Before the nominative.

(b) After the nominative.

Example: *(a)*   The *hungry* fox ran off with the goose.

           (b)   The fox, *meaning to have a fine dinner,* ran off with the goose.

EXERCISE 18

Supply an Enlargement of the Nominative:

1. The soldier told me a long story.
2. London is situated on the Thames.
3. The cow gives us good milk.
4. The farmers lead a healthy life.
5. Friends showed him kindness.
6. The trees are beautiful.
7. The horseman rode down the hill.
8. The hunter stalked his prey.
9. I will hold the foe in play.
10. Then out spake Horatius.

EXERCISE 19

Supply an Englargement of the Objective (or Accusative):
1. The cat caught mice.
2. The woodman felled the tree.
3. Jack Sprat could eat fat.
4. They admired the sun.
5. The rats have eaten corn.
6. Put on your hat.
7. I shall give you a chain.
8. The hungry fox spied grapes.
9. The sailors saw the land.
10. The skipper had taken his daughter.

EXERCISE 20

Supply Extensions of the Verb:
1. She looked.
2. The time passes.
3. They travelled.
4. The housemaid opened the door.
5. The lark was singing.
6. The little boy caught some fine fish.
7. The master scolded them.
8. We saw a great many soldiers.
9. He is the right man.
10. You must leave the house.

PART II

NOUNS

KINDS OF NOUNS

If the noun is the special name of *one* particular object it is called a PROPER NOUN.

Example: James, Mary, Saturday, February, Nairobi, Buckingham Palace.

A PROPER NOUN is always written with a CAPITAL LETTER.

A COMMON NOUN is the name of a Class of Objects, and the name is *common* to all of these objects.

Example: Pen, ink, house, machinery, ship, picture, star.

COLLECTIVE NOUNS are the names of collections or groups of things, e.g. a *pack* of cards, a *choir* of angels, a *fleet* of ships, a *herd* of cattle.

ABSTRACT NOUNS are names which do not exist except as qualities of persons or things, e.g. *height, beauty, breadth.*

Names of actions are abstract nouns, e.g. *riding, swimming, dancing.*

Both collective and abstract nouns are followed by the SINGULAR number.

The *choir* sings well.   *Riding* is my favourite hobby.

GENDER

1. Names of Males are of the MASCULINE Gender: man, lion.
2. Names of Females are of the FEMININE Gender: girl, lioness.
3. Names that can be used of Male or Female are of the COMMON Gender: child, fowl.
4. Names of things without life are of the NEUTER Gender: table, spade.

A

Feminine is *usually* formed from the masculine by adding — ess.

MASCULINE	FEMININE	MASCULINE	FEMININE
Abbot	abbess	Marquis	marchioness
Actor	actress	Master	mistress
Author	authoress	Mayor	mayoress

19

MASCULINE	FEMININE	MASCULINE	FEMININE
Duke	duchess	Murderer	murderess
Emperor	empress	Negro	negress
Giant	giantess	Patron	patroness
God	goddess	Poet	poetess
Heir	heiress	Priest	priestess
Host	hostess	Prince	princess
Hunter	huntress	Prophet	prophetess
Lion	lioness	Shepherd	shepherdess
		Tiger	tigress

B

Feminine is *often* formed from the masculine *by a Change of Word*.

MASCULINE	FEMININE	MASCULINE	FEMININE
Bachelor	spinster, maid	Gentleman	lady
Boar	sow	Stallion	mare
Boy	girl	Husband	wife
Brother	sister	King	queen
Bull	cow	Lord	lady
Cock	hen	Man	woman
Drake	duck	Nephew	niece
Earl	countess	Ram	ewe
Father	mother	Sir	madam
Friar, monk	nun	Son	daughter
Gander	goose	Uncle	aunt

C

Feminine is *sometimes* formed from the masculine *by Compound Words*.

MASCULINE	FEMININE	MASCULINE	FEMININE
Bridegroom	bride	Landlord	landlady
Grandfather	grandmother	Manservant	maidservant
He-goat	she-goat	Peacock	peahen

D

Feminine *may* be formed from the masculine *by Peculiar Changes*.

MASCULINE	FEMININE	MASCULINE	FEMININE
Fox	vixen	Sultan	sultana
Hero	heroine	Wizard	witch
Widower	widow		

NUMBER

Nouns denoting *one* thing are SINGULAR.

Nouns denoting more than one thing are PLURAL.

PLURAL is formed by adding s to singular, as:

book–s, bag–s, boy–s, pen–s, etc.

Add –es if Singular ends in a hissing sound, as: s, x, sh, ch (soft).

SINGULAR	PLURAL	SINGULAR	PLURAL
Glass	glasses	Box	boxes
Gas	gases	Fez	fezes
Grass	grasses	Brush	brushes
Mass	masses	Church	churches

If the Singular ends in y preceded by a consonant, change the y into i, and add es.

Fly	flies	Penny	pennies, pence
Cry	cries	Lady	ladies
Duty	duties	Party	parties
Army	armies		

If y is preceded by a vowel, add s.

Boy	boys	Monkey	monkeys
Day	days	Money	moneys

If Singular ends in f or fe, change f into v and add es.

Wife	wives	Leaf	leaves
Wolf	wolves	Loaf	loaves
Thief	thieves	Calf	calves
Knife	knives	Half	halves

The following simply add 's':

Chief	chiefs	Proof	proofs
Dwarf	dwarfs	Reef	reefs
Fife	fifes	Roof	roofs
Gulf	gulfs	Strife	strifes
Grief	griefs		

If Singular ends in 'o' preceded by a consonant, add 'es'.

Buffalo	buffaloes	Motto	mottoes
Cargo	cargoes	Potato	potatoes
Echo	echoes	Volcano	volcanoes
Hero	heroes		

The following simply add 's':

SINGULAR	PLURAL	SINGULAR	PLURAL
Alto	altos	Solo	solos
Halo	halos	Soprano	sopranos
Piano	pianos		

Some exceptional Plurals:

Child	children	Mouse	mice
Foot	feet	Ox	oxen
Goose	geese	Tooth	teeth
Louse	lice	Woman	women
Man	men		

Some words have alternative Plurals:

SINGULAR	PLURAL
Brother	Brothers or Brethren
Hoof	Hoofs or Hooves
Grotto	Grottos or Grottoes

Some words have Singular and Plural alike: Deer, fish, salmon, sheep, trout, cod, grouse, means, swine.

Some words used only in Plural: Bellows, spectacles, shears, scissors, thanks, trousers, tidings, tongs, victuals.

Plural of Compound Nouns: Sons-in-law, daughters-in-law, men-servants, spoonfuls, cupfuls.

EXERCISE 21

Write out the plural of the following nouns:

Hero, glory, penny, mouse, negro, key, cliff, boy, loaf, ox, knife, monarch, story, calf, valley, gas, foot, muff, church, deer, stomach, roof, brush, half, cargo, tooth, duty, monkey, lady, salmon, parent, sheep, potato, woman, volcano, thief, child, piano, baby, echo.

CASE

When we analyse the sentence, *Cats catch mice*, we say that *'Cats'* is the Nominative. It is the name of the thing we are speaking about (see page 12). We now say that it is in the NOMINATIVE CASE, and that it is Nominative to the verb 'catch'.

The Complement, when a noun or pronoun, is in the Nominative Case. In the example, 'London is a great city' (page 14), *city* and *London* refer to the same thing, and, therefore, we say that *city* is in the NOMINATIVE CASE after *is*.

In the example (page 12) 'Cats catch mice', we said that *mice* was the Object. Now, the Object is always in the OBJECTIVE CASE, and we say, then, that *mice* is in the OBJECTIVE CASE by the verb *catch*.

The Objective Case is sometimes called the Accusative.

Look at the phrase '*in the barn*'. We say that *barn* is in the Objective Case after the preposition '*in*'.

Two parts of speech, Verbs and Prepositions, put or govern a noun in the Objective Case.

EXERCISE 22

Turn back now to Exercises 13, 14, 15, 16 and 17.

Rapidly analyse the sentence and then write the case of the nouns, the Nominatives in one column and the Objectives in another.

When we use the phrase '*the boy's pencil*', we mean that the boy possessed a pencil, and, therefore, we say that 'boy's' is in the POSSESSIVE CASE.

This case is formed by adding an apostrophe, and s, if required **'s,** to the word.

The dress of the *girl*	—	the *girl's* dress.
The hat of their *father*	—	their *father's* hat.
The farm of his *uncles*	—	his *uncles'* farm.
The hoofs of the *horses*	—	the *horses'* hoofs.
The dress of the *lady*	—	the *lady's* dress.
The room of the *ladies*	—	the *ladies'* room.
The pipes of the *men*	—	the *men's* pipes.

We may state the Rule in another way. Add **'s** to the Singular Nouns and to those Plural Nouns which do not end in s.

Example:

SINGULAR	PLURAL
man's	men's
woman's	women's
child's	children's

If the Plural ends in **s**, then simply add the apostrophe:

SINGULAR	PLURAL
the horse's head	the horses' heads
the mistress's dog	the mistresses' dogs
the lady's collars	the ladies' collars
my niece's books	my nieces' books
his nephew's pony	his nephews' ponies

EXERCISE 23

Write out the following phrases in the plural:

The cow's tail, the child's toy, the bird's wing, the dog's leg, the hero's medal, the father's son, the poet's song, the girl's hands, my aunt's cat, his friend's house, our niece's letters, the monkey's tail, the woman's husband, the lady's ring.

EXERCISE 24

Copy the following, putting in the apostrophe where necessary:

1. The boys book was in his bag.
2. The shop window was full of childrens toys.
3. The boys maps were well done.
4. Wrapped in his seamans coat was he.
5. The snow was the soldiers winding-sheet.
6. The dogs kennels were near the stables.
7. James saw ten birds nests to-day.
8. The horses tails were decked with ribbons.
9. Henrys books are lying on the desk.
10 A mouses skin is very soft.
11 His voice was like a lions.
12 Two brothers and a sister visited their aunts farm.
    The boys great desire was to get up on the horses backs, but the girl liked to gather the hens eggs and to bring some home in her mothers pretty basket.

EXERCISE 25

Make sentences using the following words in the Possessive Case:

Brother, boys, companion, woman, enemy, cousin, ladies, traveller, teacher, servants, soldier, judge, workman, sergeant, women, children, sailors, milliner, pony, baker, elephant, shepherd.

PRONOUNS

PERSONAL PRONOUNS have three *persons*.

1st	The person speaking:	I, me, we, ours.
2nd	The person spoken to:	You, yours.
3rd	The person spoken about:	He, she, it, they them.

Note: Nouns are used only in 2nd and 3rd persons.

	1ST PERSON			2ND PERSON	
	SING.	PLUR.		SING.	PLUR.
Nom.,	I	we	*Nom.,*	thou	you
Poss.,	mine	ours	*Poss.,*	thine	yours
Obj.,	me	us	*Obj.,*	thee	you

3RD PERSON

	SINGULAR			PLURAL
	MASC.	FEM.	NEUT.	
Nom.,	he	she	it	they
Poss.,	his	hers	its	theirs
Obj.,	him	her	it	them

Note: The following are called POSSESSIVE ADJECTIVES:
My, our, thy, your, his, her, its, their.

Note: The following are called POSSESSIVE PRONOUNS:
Mine, ours; thine, yours; his, hers; its, theirs.

Note: Pronouns in the Possessive Case never have an apostrophe. **Its, ours, yours** — not it's, your's. It's is the shortened version of it is.

A Pronoun which acts both as a Pronoun and a Conjunction is called a RELATIVE PRONOUN. The noun to which it relates is called its ANTECEDENT. A Relative Pronoun agrees with its antecedent in Number and Person, but not in Case.

The RELATIVE PRONOUNS are:
Who, whose, whom, which, what (that which) that, as.

'As' is used as a Pronoun only after *'same'* and *'such'*,

Nom., ... who
Poss., ... whose
Obj., ... whom

'Who', 'whose' and 'whom' refer to persons only. 'Which' refers to animals and things.

Note: Some Pronouns may be treated as possessive Adjectives.

PRONOUN	ADJECTIVE
This book is *his*	This is *his* book
Each got her share	*Each* girl received a gift

EXERCISE 26

Pick out the Pronouns, Personal and Relative, and give their Person, Number and Case.

1. They found the man who had lost himself.
2. I do not know what he means.
3. Do you know whose knife this is?
4. Which is the way to the nearest farm?
5. We have not seen them to-day.
6. I know it quite well, but I forget its name.
7. This is better than yours.
8. Who brought the message?
9. Here is the boy that you want.
10. A child whose parents are dead, is an orphan.
11. This book is not theirs.
12. This is the same book as yours.
13. Of whom did he speak?
14. Each must do his duty.
15. Everyone received a prize.

VERBS

A VERB is a word by which we make a statement or ask a question.

Turn to page 12 and examine the sentence, 'Cats catch mice'.

The verb *'catch'* tells us what the cats do, but the action does not remain with the cats, but *passes over* to the mice.

The verb *'catch'* is TRANSITIVE (passing over). In a Transitive Verb the action is not confined to the 'doer' or Nominative, but takes effect on something else. It governs the Objective Case.

Rule: **A Transitive Verb always has an object, but an Intransitive Verb, never.**

Now take the sentence: 'The boy walked slowly away'.

The action expressed by *'walked'* remains with the 'doer', and does not pass over to anything else. It is, therefore, called an INTRANSITIVE VERB.

Note: The action of an Intransitive Verb is one of motion or rest.

Some Transitive Verbs are used Intransitively.

The guard *stopped* the train (trans.).
The train *stopped* at the station (intrans.).

These verbs must be called Transitive or Intransitive according to their use in a sentence.

TRANSITIVE	INTRANSITIVE
He *boils* the water	The water *boils*
They *bathe* the child	They *bathe* in the river
They *open* the doors at nine	School *opens* at nine o'clock
He *broke* a window	The waves *broke* on the shore
She *sets* the girls in order	The sun *sets* in the west

Exercise 27

Pick out the Verbs, and tell whether they are Transitive or Intransitive.

1.   The cat sat by the fireside.
2.   They found an old well in the garden.
3.   The dog caught a rabbit.
4.   The two boys ran home.
5.   The driver came in all covered with snow.
6.   The fisherman caught some fine fish.
7.   The waves broke over the ship.
8.   Out rang the rifle shot.
9.   It shivered the window.
10.   The master taught the boy.
11.   He teaches for a living.

27

12. It was raining heavily when we came in.
13. The leading man burst the door open.
14. The storm burst violently upon us.
15. The sun rises in the east.
16. The lumbermen fell the trees with axes.
17. Peter's books lay on the table.
18. Our hens lay very large eggs.

TENSE refers to the time in which an action takes place. These are three tenses — PRESENT, PAST, FUTURE.

TO ARRIVE

	SINGULAR	PLURAL
PRESENT	1. I arrive	We arrive
	2. Thou arrivest	You arrive
	3. He arrives	They arrive
PAST	1. I arrived	We arrived
	2. Thou arrivedst	You arrived
	3. He arrived	They arrived
FUTURE	1. I shall arrive	We shall arrive
	2. Thou wilt arrive	You will arrive
	3. He will arrive	They will arrive

TO BE

	SINGULAR	PLURAL
PRESENT	1. I am	We are
	2. Thou art	You are
	3. He is	They are
PAST	1. I was	We were
	2. Thou wast (were)	You were
	3. He was	They were
FUTURE	1. I shall be	We shall be
	2. Thou wilt be	You will be
	3. He will be	They will be

TO HAVE

	SINGULAR	PLURAL
PRESENT	1. I have 2. Thou hast 3. He has	We have You have They have
PAST	1. I had 2. Thou hadst 3. He had	We had You had They had
FUTURE	1. I shall have 2. Thou wilt have 3. He will have	We shall have You will have They will have

Those verbs which we have just learned agree with a Nominative, and are called FINITE VERBS.

Note: The 3rd person singular present tense ends in 's'.

On page 11 we had an example of the same thing being told in two different ways.

(a) The boy broke the window.
(b) The window was broken by the boy.

In *(a)* the Nominative is the 'doer' of the action, and the verb is, therefore, said to be ACTIVE.

In *(b)* the Nominative is the sufferer of the action, and the verb is, therefore, said to be PASSIVE.

Note: The *object* of the Active form becomes the *subject* of the Passive form, and also note that only *Transitive Verbs* can become *Passive*.

EXERCISE 28

(a) Turn the following sentences from the Active to the Passive:
1. The boy kicked the ball.
2. Mary loved her little doll.
3. The gamekeeper caught a fine salmon.
4. The visitors admired our pictures.
5. The shepherd watches his sheep.

29

6. That little spark kindled a great fire.
7. The empty vessel makes the greatest sound.
8. We met a little bare-footed girl.
9. They did not utter a sound.
10. Then an open field they crossed.

EXERCISE 29

(b) Turn the following sentences from the Passive to the Active:
1. The plate was broken by a servant.
2. The book was read by the little girl.
3. The men were ordered to go away by the policeman.
4. The ripening corn was destroyed by the storm.
5. A fine big tree was split by lightning.
6. A chimney was set on fire by our neighbours.
7. Grammar is liked by most pupils.
8. This book will be returned by us.
9. The man was assisted to a more comfortable position.
10. We were astonished at his action.

CONJUGATION

1. English Verbs may form their Past Tense and Past Participle by adding **d**, **ed** or **t**, to the Present.

PRESENT	PAST	PAST PARTICIPLE
arrive	arrive*d*	arrive*d*
Command	command*ed*	command*ed*
telegraph	telegraph*ed*	telegraph*ed*
Bend	bent	bent

These verbs are known as WEAK VERBS.

2. Some verbs form their past tense by changing their vowel sound.

PRESENT	PAST	PAST PARTICIPLE
Ring	rang	rung
Blow	blew	blown

These verbs are known as STRONG VERBS and are usually Old English verbs.

3. Verbs which have the same form for all three parts are usually weak.

PRESENT	PAST	PAST PARTICIPLE
Burst	burst	burst
hurt	hurt	hurt

4. There are certain irregular formations, e.g.:

go	went	gone

Pick out the strong and weak verbs in the following list.

PRESENT	PAST	PAST PARTICIPLE
Am	was	been
Arise	arose	arisen
Awake	awoke	awoke (awakened)
Bear	bore	borne
Beat	beat	beaten
Become	became	become
Begin	began	begun
Behold	beheld	beheld
Bend	bent	bent
Bind	bound	bound
Bite	bit	bitten, bit
Blow	blew	blown
Bleed	bled	bled
Break	broke	broken
Bring	brought	brought
Build	built	built
Burn	burnt, burned	burnt, burned
Burst	burst	burst
Buy	bought	bought
Catch	caught	caught
Choose	chose	chosen
Cling	clung	clung
Come	came	come
Cost	cost	cost
Creep	crept	crept
Cut	cut	cut

31

PRESENT	PAST	PAST PARTICIPLE
Dig	dug	dug
Do	did	done
Draw	drew	drawn
Drink	drank	drunk
Drive	drove	driven
Dwell	dwelt	dwelt
Eat	ate	eaten
Fall	fell	fallen
Feel	felt	felt
Feed	fed	fed
Find	found	found
Fight	fought	fought
Flee	fled	fled
Fling	flung	flung
Fly	flew	flown
Forget	forgot	forgotten
Forsake	forsook	forsaken
Freeze	froze	frozen
Get	got	got
Give	gave	given
Go	went	gone
Grind	ground	ground
Grow	grew	grown
Hear	heard	heard
Hide	hid	hid, hidden
Hit	hit	hit
Hold	held	held
Hurt	hurt	hurt
Keep	kept	kept
Kneel	knelt	knelt
Know	knew	known
Lay	laid	laid
Lead	led	led
Leave	left	left
Lend	lent	lent

PRESENT	PAST	PAST PARTICIPLE
Let	let	let
Lie	lay	lain
Lose	lost	lost
Make	made	made
Meet	met	met
Pay	paid	paid
Put	put	put
Read	read	read
Ride	rode	ridden
Ring	rang	rung
Run	ran	run
Say	said	said
See	saw	seen
Seek	sought	sought
Sell	sold	sold
Send	sent	sent
Set	set	set
Sew	sewed	sewn, sowed
Shake	shook	shaken
Shine	shone	shone
Shoot	shot	shot
Show	showed	shown
Shut	shut	shut
Sing	sang	sung
Sink	sank	sunk
Sit	sat	sat
Slay	slew	slain
Sleep	slept	slept
Slide	slid	slid
Slink	slunk	slunk
Slit	slit	slit
Smite	smote	smitten
Spell	spelt	spelt
Speak	spoke	spoken
Spend	spent	spent
Spill	spilt	spilt

PRESENT	PAST	PAST PARTICIPLE
Spin	spun	spun
Split	split	split
Spread	spread	spread
Spring	sprang	sprung
Stand	stood	stood
Steal	stole	stolen
Stick	stuck	stuck
Sting	stung	stung
Strike	struck	struck
Strive	strove	striven
Swear	swore	sworn
Swell	swelled	swollen
Sweep	swept	swept
Swim	swam	swum
Swing	swung	swung
Take	took	taken
Teach	taught	taught
Tell	told	told
Think	thought	thought
Tread	trod	trodden
Wear	wore	worn
Weave	wove	woven
Win	won	won
Wind	wound	wound
Wring	wrung	wrung
Write	wrote	written
Can	could	*(wanting)*
May	might	*(wanting)*
Shall	should	*(wanting)*
Will	would	*(wanting)*

The Present Participle of a verb is formed by adding –ing,
   e.g. I was rising.
Hence, 'I was standing' and *not*, as is said in some places, 'I was stood'.
Similarly correct are: I was sitting.
                             I was kneeling.
                             I was lying.

ADJECTIVES

An Adjective is a word which describes or qualifies a Noun or Pronoun.

AN is used before a Noun beginning with a vowel sound or a mute 'h': an oasis, an orange, an heir.

A is used before a Noun beginning with a consonant: a book, a banana.

THE is always an Adjective.

THIS and THAT are the only Adjectives that have a plural form.

SING.	PLUR.
this	these
that	those

COMPARISON OF ADJECTIVES

In the sentences,

(a) This is a *large* house,

(b) James is a *clever* boy,

the adjectives 'large' and 'clever' express a simple quality, and we say they are POSITIVE DEGREE.

If we say, 'This is a *larger* house than that', *'larger'* expresses a greater degree of size than large. Then we say *'larger'* is COMPARATIVE DEGREE. In the same way, if we *compare* James with another boy, we might say James is *cleverer* than Robert; *'cleverer'* is Comparative degree.

Make a sentence with an adjective of more than two syllables.

'This is a beautiful picture'.

Now make a sentence expressing a greater degree of beauty.

'This picture is *more beautiful* than that'.

'More beautiful' is comparative. Notice that we use the Comparative when **two** things are compared.

Now, if we want to express a still greater degree of beauty, we say,

'This is the *most beautiful* picture in the room'.

We are now comparing the picture with all other pictures in the room, and we say that *'most beautiful'* is SUPERLATIVE DEGREE.

If the Adjective is a small word like *'clever'*, we say the Superlative is *'cleverest'*, as:

William is the *cleverest* boy in the class.

THE COMPARATIVE DEGREE **is formed by adding** ER **or the Adverb** MORE **to the Positive, and is used when comparing one thing with another.**

THE SUPERLATIVE DEGREE **is formed by adding** EST **or the Adverb** MOST **to the Positive, and is used when comparing one thing with two or several other things.**

POSITIVE	COMPARATIVE	SUPERLATIVE
Small	smaller	smallest
Bold	bolder	boldest
Long	longer	longest
Gay	gayer	gayest
Thin	thinner	thinnest
Red	redder	reddest
Sad	sadder	saddest
Worthy	worthier	worthiest

IRREGULAR COMPARISONS

POSITIVE	COMPARATIVE	SUPERLATIVE
Bad	worse	worst
Good	better	best
Little	less	least
Much	more	most
Many	more	most
Old	older	oldest
	elder	eldest
Late	later	latest
	latter	last

EXERCISE 30

Compare:

Loud, good, red, rich, pretty, large, late, tall, short, clever, mountainous, old, splendid, calm, strange, bad, beautiful, sweet, guilty, able, noble, handsome, manly, faithful, free, wide, little, rude.

EXERCISE 31

Make sentences using the Adjectives in Exercise 30.
(a) in the Positive, (b) in the Comparative, and (c) in the Superlative degree.

ADVERBS

An Adverb describes or modifies any Part of Speech except a Noun or Pronoun.

Most Adverbs are formed from Adjectives by adding **–ly**.

ADJECTIVE	ADVERB
Wise	wisely
True	truly

COMPARISON OF ADVERBS

Adverbs may be compared in the same way as Adjectives.

Example:

POSITIVE	COMPARATIVE	SUPERLATIVE
Fast	fast*er*	fast*est*
Late	lat*er*	lat*est*
Quickly	more quickly	most quickly
Slowly	more slowly	most slowly

In some Adverbs the comparative forms are irregular:

Well	better	best
Much	more	most
Little	less	least
Badly	worse	worst
Far	farther	farthest

EXERCISE 32

Make sentences using the Adverbs:

Firmly, quickly, strongly, fast, slowly, prettily, daintily, truthfully, comfortably, sadly, often, perfectly, easily, well, nearly, lovely, completely, soon, profitably, sharply, politely, ably, gaily, happily, far.

PREPOSITIONS

A PREPOSITION shows the relation between one thing and another.

A Preposition links words together.

The lady stepped *into* the car.

Into links car with stepped.

The dog ran *after* the sheep.

He passed *through* the door.

37

Prepositions govern the Objective Case or Accusative Case.

The Preposition must not be confused with the Adverb.

The only way to distinguish them is to see what *work* each does. (See page 9.)

ADVERB	PREPOSITION
He went *below*.	He sat *below* the pulpit.
I saw him *before*.	He stood *before* the judge.
Come *in*.	He was *in* the room.
They sat *inside*.	The book was *inside* the box.

EXERCISE 33

Make sentences, using the Prepositions:

Into, beyond, to, through, on, by, with, over, under, for, from, around, near, at, of, about, past, besides, within, between, till, during, until, against, behind, like, opposite, beneath, towards.

———————

CONJUNCTIONS

A Conjunction is a word used for joining *words* **or** *sentences*.

When it joins words it always joins similar Parts of Speech, i.e. Noun with Noun, Adjective with Adjective, etc.

Margaret and *Jean* were good friends.

She was *rich* and *generous*.

The boy was *poor* but *honest*.

When a Conjunction joins sentences to make one larger sentence, we call the sentences Clauses.

The girl was intelligent *and* she made progress.

The boy was clever, *but* he was very lazy.

He could not win *though* he played his best.

He was paid *after* his work was done.

The Conjunction should not be confused with the Preposition.

PREPOSITION	CONJUNCTION
He worked *till* ten o'clock.	He worked *till* it was ten o'clock.
She went away *before* dinner.	She went away *before* dinner was served.
He locked the door *after* them.	He locked the door *after* they had gone.

38

EXERCISE 34

(a) *Pick out Conjunctions:*

He came early, but he did not avoid the crush.
The enemy entered the village and burned many houses.
The old man went to bed because he felt tired.
The man dug up the treasure before the others came.
I do not know why they did not come.
He was so badly hurt that he died.
She could not remember where she laid the book.
She will play if she is asked.
We heard that the King had arrived.
You must play the game, or leave the field.
If he does that again, he will be dismissed.
When they returned, they were covered with mud.
He spoke to me, while he was waiting for his train.
As he came along the street, he observed some new shops.

EXERCISE 35

(b) *Make sentences, using the following Conjunctions:*
Because, that, when, if, while, as, but, and, how, or, nor, until,
for, although.

PARSING

Along Scotia's hills shot up the beacon fires.

Along	Prep. gov. hills.
Scotia's	Noun prop. possess. 'hills' 3rd pers. sing. neut.
hills	Noun com., 3rd pers. pl., neut., obj. by along
shot	Verb, intr. past, 3rd pers. pl., agrees with fires.
up	Adv. manner, mod. shot.
the	Adj. point out fires.
beacon	Adj. describ. fires.
fires	Noun, com., 3rd pers. pl. neut., nom. to shot.

In parsing such forms of the Verb as *'will have arrived'*, *'has been coming'*, etc., it will be simpler for pupils to parse each word separately.

The first verb agrees with the Nominative in *person* and *number*.

39

To have takes after it the *Past Participle*.

To be takes after it the *Past Participle* or *Present Participle*.

Other Verbs take after them the *Present Infinitive*.

Note that the *Present Participle* is formed by adding *–ing* to the Present, as: 'come', 'coming', and also that the *Present Infinitive* is the form of the Verb with *to* before it, as, 'to come', 'to run'. After certain Verbs *'to'* is omitted.

In the phrase, *'will have arrived'*, *'will'* agrees with the Nominative, *'have'* is the Present Infinitive, and *'arrived'* is Past Participle.

In the phrase, *'has been coming'*, *'has'* agrees with the Nominative, *'been'* is Past Participle, and *'coming'* is Present Participle.

THE SAME WORD USED AS DIFFERENT PARTS OF SPEECH

His	*Poss. Pron.*	— This book is not *his*.
	Poss. Adj.	— *His* book was found yesterday.
This	*Adj.*	— *This* brooch is very pretty.
	Pron.	— *This* is my brooch.
Village	*Noun*	— He lived in a quaint old *village*.
	Adj.	— All the *village* children were present.
More	*Adj.*	— *More* men will be required.
	Adv.	— She is *more* diligent than her sister.
Each	*Adj.*	— The captain selected *each* boy carefully.
	Pron.	— *Each* was chosen according to his ability.
Round.	*Prep.*	— The boy ran *round* the corner.
	Adv.	— The bird flew *round* and *round*.
	Noun	— The sentry walks his lonely *round*.
	Verb	— Gama was the first to *round* the Cape of Good Hope.
That	*Adj.*	— Give me *that* book.
	Pron.	— Where did you find *that*?
	Conj.	— I did not know *that* he was so smart.

PRINCIPAL AND SUBORDINATE CLAUSES

The sentences in Exercises 13 – 17 have all had only **one subject** and **one predicate**, and, therefore, they are called **Simple** sentences.

Let us take two Simple Sentences.

'The girl was intelligent.'
'The girl made progress.'

Join them by means of the conjunction *'and'*. 'The girl was intelligent and she made progress.' The two sentences thus combined are called Clauses. As each in itself makes complete sense, they are said to be *independent* of each other.

Clauses that are connected by a conjunction are not always independent.

'The man was paid after the work was done.'

We find that the clause 'The man was paid' can by itself make complete sense, therefore it is **Independent**. The clause 'after the work was done' does not make complete sense when taken alone, but it depends upon the first clause. We call it, therefore, a **Dependent** clause.

Example:

(a) The girl was intelligent   Independent Clause.
(and) she made progress.   Independent Clause.

(b) The man was paid   Independent Clause.
(after) the work was done.   Dependent Clause.

A Clause, whether Independent or Dependent *always* **contains a verb.**

EXERCISE 36

Pick out the Clauses, and say whether they are Independent or Dependent.

1. The boy came to the door and handed in a letter.
2. The girl played with her doll when her lessons were finished.
3. When I arrived at the station, the train had gone.
4. He would help me if he could.
5. I know where you laid the book.
6. The boy was clever, but he was lazy.

41

7. I came, I saw, I conquered.
8. He did not utter a word as they drove along.
9. When I looked from the hotel window, up the river came a swift boat.
10. The farmer caught the boy stealing apples.
11. As the boy crossed the field, he saw a hare.
12. Do you know where Robert Burns was born?
13. I have found the book which you lost yesterday.
14. They promised that they would come.
15. Crossing to the other side of the street, he gazed up at a window.
16. He was so tired that he could not work.
17. The man was very old, yet he was quite strong.
18. The message boy came along the road, whistling merrily.
19. They toil not, neither do they spin.

Each *Independent Clause* is usually called a PRINCIPAL CLAUSE.

Each *Dependent Clause* is called a SUBORDINATE CLAUSE.

1. **If a sentence contains** *one subject and one predicate*, **it is called a Simple Sentence.**

2. **If a sentence contains** *two or more Principal clauses*, **it is called a Compound Sentence.**

3. **If a sentence contains** *one Principal* **and** *one or more Subordinate clauses*, **it is called a Complex Sentence.**

EXERCISE 37

1. *Go over the previous exercise, using the names Principal and Subordinate, and also tell whether the sentence is Simple, Compound or Complex.*

2. *Make sentences of your own, pointing out which clauses are Principal and which are Subordinate, and then tell whether the sentence is Simple, Compound or Complex.*

COMPLEX SENTENCES

'The miller wore a *white* hat.'

'White' is an adjective describing hat.

Expand 'white' into a clause, and the clause becomes 'The miller wore a hat *which was white*'.

The clause, 'which was white', describes hat, and, therefore, is called an ADJECTIVE CLAUSE

Note: **An adjective clause always describes a *word* in some *other clause*.**

EXERCISE 38

Turn the following Adjectives or Adjectival phrases into Adjective Clauses:

1 I like a *sharp* knife.
2 The boy caught a *tame* rabbit.
3 A *wise* man is happy.
4 Near the river we found a rod *lying on the ground*.
5 I do not like his way *of speaking*.
6 We know a man *named* Smith.
7 The *thirsty* boy took a big drink.
8 From the hills came a shepherd *with his weary flocks*.
9 Sweet is the month *of blooming roses*.
10 The porter, *hearing a noise*, ran to the door.
11 The *rich* man came to his aid.
12 The man *with plenty of money* paid all expenses.

EXERCISE 39

Supply an Adjective Clause:

1 I know a river _____ .
2 The doctor _____ is his cousin.
3 The tree _____ was struck by lightning.
4 The noise _____ was like the sound of thunder.
5 The boy _____ was punished.
6 I remember the house _____ .
7. He told me a story _____ .

8. The girl could not tell the reason _____ .
   (*Note:* Why = for which.)
9. The house _____ is a very beautiful one.
10. In Stratford I saw the house _____ .
11. The reason _____ was that he was sick.
12. The girl could not do the exercise _____ .
13. Find out the time _____ . (*Note:* When = at which.)
14. Can you tell me the name of the boy _____ ?

EXERCISE 40

Pick out the Adjective Clause:

1. The soldier who deserted, was captured.
2. Here is a chair which is worth five pounds.
3. There is the boy whose cap you found.
4. The excuse which he gave was reasonable.
5. The field in which we played, has been ploughed.
6. I remember the house where I was born.
7. The lady who lost her fan called this morning.
8. The cottage where Burns was born is in Alloway.
9. She remembers the place where they saw the man.
10. The book he found belonged to my cousin.
11. His niece of whom he was very fond was married to-day.
12. The lady who gave the treat to the children, lives in this neighbourhood.
13. The evil that men do lives after them.
14. Show me the umbrella you bought.
15. The ship in which we sailed was very comfortable.
16. The guide we had was very intelligent.
17. The sergeant gave the signal to the men, who then opened fire.
18. The cattle that strayed among the corn belonged to Farmer Giles.
19. Tell me the reason why you were late.
20. The time when the ship sails is not yet fixed.

'We rise early.'

'Early' is an Adverb modifying 'rise'.

Expand 'early' into a phrase, and we have

'We rise *at six in the morning*.'

Expand 'early' into a clause, and we have

'We rise *when the clock strikes six*.'

'When the clock strikes six' modifies 'rise'. It is called, therefore, an ADVERB CLAUSE.

Note: **An Adverb Clause always modifies a word in some other Clause.**

EXERCISE 41

Turn the following Adverbs and Adverbial Phrases into Clauses:
1. The cows were sold *in the market*.
2. I will come *willingly*.
3. He made friends *everywhere*.
4. I shall come *presently*.
5. The class will be dismissed *at the end of the lesson*.
6. They will meet him *on his arrival*.
7. I wrote the letter *at his request*.
8. *On your return* take this book to him.
9. *Wearily* he sat down.
10. I shall wait *till four o'clock*.

EXERCISE 42

Supply Adverbial Clauses:
1. He was standing at the door _____ .
2. She wandered into the wood _____ .
3. _____ they imagined themselves safe.
4. The old man laid down his bundle _____ .
5. _____ we found the train had gone.
6. The boy did not come to school _____ .
7. He rose up _____ .
8. _____ my brother paid me a visit.
9. The master was so pleased with the boy _____ .
10. The boy gave the monkey some nuts _____ .
11. I shall wait here _____ .

12. He had gone _____ .
13. You may return the book _____ .
14. _____ he sat down.
15. He said that he could not buy the horse _____ .

ANALYSIS

EXERCISE 43

Pick out the Adverb Clauses:

1. The tree lay where it fell.
2. The boys rushed out when the bell rang.
3. The horse came to me because I had some corn.
4. The Egyptians were a great people before the Romans ruled the world.
5. If I have time, I shall come to see you.
6. He tried many times before he succeeded.
7. They gave him a prize that he might work harder in future.
8. Unless they leave at once, they will be too late.
9. When the policeman arrived, the thief had escaped.
10. He stepped forward carefully lest he should fall.
11. She is honest though she is poor.
12. The gardener works as he pleases.
13. The poor fellow was so tired that he fell asleep.
14. We must go home, as it is growing dark.
15. When the cat's away, the mice will play.
16. Nairobi is larger than Mombasa (is).
17. As he came into the room, he perceived a stranger.
18. The problem was so difficult that it could not be solved.
19. Although he has riches, he is not content.
20. If you wish to preserve your life, keep perfectly still.

NOUN CLAUSE

He said 'something'.

'Something' is a Noun, Objective by said.

Turn 'something' into a clause, and we have:

He said, 'he would play with us.'

'He would play with us' does the same work as 'something', and, therefore, it is a NOUN CLAUSE Objective by 'said'.

46

This 'book' belongs to him.

'Book' is a noun Nominative to belongs.

'What I have in my hand', belongs to him.

'What I have in my hand' does the same work as 'book'. It is then a NOUN CLAUSE Nominative to 'belongs'.

A Noun Clause may be Nominative to or Objective by a verb.

Note: A Noun Clause is always Objective by or Nominative to a *word* in some *other Clause*.

EXERCISE 44

Turn the following Nouns and Noun Phrases into Clauses:
1. The traveller told me a *story*.
2. We advised him *to go home*.
3. They admitted *having made a mistake*.
4. He told us the *result of the match*.
5. Mary told Jane a *secret*.
6. The captain *demanded obedience*.
7. *His error* was made plain to him.

EXERCISE 45

Supply Noun Clauses.
1. The boy told me _____ .
2. He is very anxious to know _____ .
3. I cannot believe _____ .
4. _____ is quite certain.
5. The master knows very well _____ .
6. The hope _____ spurred him on.
7. It is my opinion _____ .
8. Will you tell me _____ ?
9 I wish to know _____ .
10 I fear _____ .
11 _____ was the question.
12 _____ asked the father?

EXERCISE 46

Pick out the Noun Clauses.
1. I do not know why he did that.
2. He thinks that he has done very well.

47

3. The traveller described how he shot the tiger.
4. You may be sure he will not do that again.
5. I could not tell where he had gone.
6. He confessed that he had made a sad mistake.
7. Tell me how many mistakes you have made.
8. What he did with the money we shall never know.
9. Our greatest desire is that we shall succeed.
10. I told him when he could meet me.
11. Where he was going was unknown to anyone.
12. Why he came I do not know.

GENERAL ANALYSIS

Can you tell me where I shall find the man who takes charge of the baggage?

COMPLEX SENTENCE

CLAUSE	KIND	RELATION
1. Can you tell me	Prin. cl.	
2. Where I shall find the man	Sub. noun cl.	obj. by can tell
3. Who takes charge of the baggage	Sub. adj. cl.	qual. man

The night was perfectly still, and the whole palace was wrapped in a profound quiet that was almost oppressive.

COMPOUND SENTENCE

CLAUSE	KIND	RELATION
1. The night was perfectly still	Prin. cl.	
2. And the whole palace was wrapped in a profound quiet	Princ. cl.	
3. That was almost oppressive	Sub. adj. cl.	qual. quiet.

EXERCISE 47

Analyse:

1. I have spoken to a man who proudly wore the Victoria Cross.
2. The gardener will fell the tree and lay out the borders.
3. The pirates sank the vessel which had fallen into their hands.
4. I know a place where we can have some very fine oranges.
5. When he was accused, he confessed that he had broken the ruler.
6. We asked him when he intended to do the work.
7. The boy you met when you were coming home, lost his cap at school.
8. He failed because he did not take sufficient care.
9. They ran very fast so that they might reach the station in time.
10. The house stands on the landing-place, to which we steered our boat when we returned from the island.
11. I am uneasy because I know that he will be exposed to great danger, if he goes on that journey.
12. The weather was so stormy that the steamer could not cross the channel which separates the island from the mainland.
13. The dogs did bark, the children screamed, up flew the windows all.
14. After his house had been thoroughly examined, his innocence was proved, and he regained his popularity.
15. Without another word, she lifted up the astonished man, threw him across her shoulders, and carried him to a place of safety.
16. On the hill which faces the farm, I notice that a wood has been planted since I was here last.
17. When I looked from the hotel window, up the river came a swift boat.
18. If you come with me, I will tell you a good story I heard.
19. But as I approached I perceived he was fully armed.
20. Sailing down the river, we observed on each bank traces of the enemy's presence.
21. As the boy crossed the field, he saw the tree which had been blown over.
22. As the weather is warm, I think I shall go to the sea-side, where the cool breezes blow.
23. The people shouted 'God Save the Queen', when they saw the carriage which was drawn by six white horses.

24. If the minister speaks, I believe we shall have a capital address.
25. When we arrived at the station, we found that the train was crowded with passengers.
26. If the boy is very clever, I think he will get the prize.
27. When the guns that were guarding our trenches ceased firing, our men advanced.
28. If you come with me, I shall show you the house where I lived when I was a boy.
29. How the men who had preceded us, had passed the sentinels, we could not imagine.
30. When Napoleon was crossing the Alps, the cannon were placed on rough sledges, which were drawn by soldiers over the mountain passes.
31. It is said that in those desolate regions which are winter-bound during the greater part of the year, man plays an insignificant part.
32. If you ask me, I shall show you where I lost the purse yesterday.
33. They asked him whether he was guilty, but he refused to answer till he had consulted his agent.
34. When I met your father, I asked him where he was going.
35. When they saw the clouds of smoke approaching, the soldiers at once suspected that the enemy was trying a new plan.
36. When we came down the street together, he told me who had sung at the concert the night before.
37. As I walked through this valley, I perceived it was strewn with diamonds which were of a surpassing size.
38. His change of residence was of little advantage, for the camp was scarcely quiet for the night, before he shrieked out that the black cats were there.

1. *Analyse and parse words in italics:*

   As I did not know when he *went away*, I did not manage to see *him*.

2. *Analyse and parse words in italics:*

   When I *was going* home last night, I *met* the man you *saw* in Paris last summer.

3. *Analyse:*

While we came down the street *together*, he told me *who* had sung at the concert the night *before*.

Tell parts of speech of words in *italics*, and give pres. infin. of all the verbs.

4. *Analyse:*

But as I came nearer, I perceived presently that he had a bow and arrow.

Grammar to be done orally.

5. As the weather is warm, I think I shall go to the sea-side where the cool breezes blow.

   (i) How many clauses are in the sentence?
   (ii) What is the principal verb?
   (iii) What kind of clause is 'as the weather is warm'?
   (iv) What kind of clause is 'where the cool breezes blow'?
   (v) What tense is 'shall go'?

6. When we arrived at the station, we found that the train was late.

   (i) How many clauses are there?
   (ii) What is the verb in the principal clause?
   (iii) What kind of clause is 'that the train was late'?
   (iv) What part of speech is 'we'?
   (v) What part of speech is 'late'?

7. *Analyse and parse words in italics:*

'*Sailing* down the river we observed on *each* bank traces of the *enemy's* presence.'

8. *Analyse:*

Slowly came the weary horseman down the hill.

Parse words in *italics* in the sentence: As he was looking at the book, *he* noticed that the page *which* he was reading was *badly* stained.

9. *Analyse:*

   If the minister speaks, I believe we shall have a speech worth hearing.

   What part of speech is 'speech'. Write down the past tense of 'speaks'.

10. *Analyse:*

   As the boy crossed the field, he saw the tree which had been blown down.

   Which parts of speech are 'he', 'which' and 'down'?

11. *Analyse:*

   A man who was visiting France wrote home that he had met many of his friends.

12. *Analyse:*

   Round the room are hung several maps. The child thought that she had lost her book.

   Analyse and parse words in italics:

   They asked *him whether* he was *guilty, but* he refused *to answer* till he had consulted *his* agent.

13. *Analyse and parse words in italics:*

   On looking at *my* watch, *which* goes very *well*, I *found* that it was but six o'clock.

14. *Analyse and parse words in italics:*

   The people shouted 'God Save the Queen', when they *saw* the carriage, *which* was drawn *by* six white horses.

15. *Analyse, and tell part of speech of 'if'.*
   Write down the first pronoun and its plural:

   If you come with me, I will say you are kind.

16. *Analyse and parse words in italics:*

   While I looked from the *hotel* window, *up* the *river came* the *swift* boat.

17. *Analyse and parse words in italics:*

   As soon as the boys *entered* the hall, they saw the *boy who* was going to sing when *his* turn came.

18. *Analyse and parse words in italics:*

He was a *healthy* child till he was *nearly two* years *old*, when he *contracted* a *fever*.

19. *Analyse:*

His mother will be much consoled when she learns that her son has escaped so many dangers.

20. *Analyse and parse words in italics:*

When they saw the clouds *of* smoke *approaching*, the soldiers at once suspected *that* the enemy was trying a *new* plan.

21. *Analyse:*

On the side of the hill which faces the school, I notice that a house has been built since I was here last.

 (i) Make adjectives from 'school', and use them in a sentence.

 (ii) What part of speech is 'notice'? Make an adjective from it. Use it in a sentence.

 (iii) What part of speech is 'faces'? Can it be another part of speech? Use it so.

 (iv) What part of speech is 'since', and why?

22. *Analyse and parse words in italics:*

If *you* had arrived at the *station* a few minutes *earlier*, you would have seen the soldiers *who* were leaving for the front.

23. *Analyse:*

Each of us chewed a piece of seal's flesh to stay our hunger, having no power to swallow.

Also analyse and parse words in italics:

Breathes there the *man* with soul *so dead*,
Who never to *himself* hath said,
'This is my *own*, my native land!'

24. *Analyse and parse words in italics:*

When the young *folks* arrived, the lady said *that* she was glad *to see* them.

25. *Analyse:*

When I return from the town, I shall tell you how the game was played.

26. *Analyse and parse words in italics:*

If he *took that* route, he expected that he would have *to fight* his way through powerful *tribes*.

27. *Analyse:*

His listless length at noontide he would stretch and pore upon the brook that babbles by.

Part of speech of 'length'. What adjective comes from it?

Part of speech of 'that'. Make a sentence using it as another part of speech.

28. *Analyse and tell parts of speech of words in italics:*

Boys and girls *who* do not *like* singing, will be *very* glad *when this* song is over.

29. *Analyse and parse words in italics:*

When I asked the *boy* if he *was better*, he said he was.

Define a principal clause and subordinate clause.

State kinds of subordinate clauses, and kinds of adverbial clauses.

30. *Analyse and parse words in italics:*

As *we* were *now* to hold *up* our heads a *little* higher in the *world*, my friend *suggested* we should sell the colt.

Oral questions on gender and person of pronouns.

31. *Analyse and tell parts of speech of words in italics:*

If he does not return soon, *we* must send *for* the *message* boy *who* left *this* parcel.

32. *Analyse and parse words in italics:*

When I *met* the boy, he asked me when I had seen his *father*.

33. *Analyse:*

I have seen the kingly chase run through the deep glades which follow the stream.

34. *Analyse:*

The farmer could not find out who it was that opened the gate and allowed the cattle to wander.

Parse 'that', and name the subject of the verb 'allowed'.

35. *Analyse:*

My friend, who told the story as he sat beside his hearthstone in his English home, now paused.

Part of speech of who, as, beside, now.

Case of — friend, who, hearthstone, home.

36. *Analyse:*

One French author, who lived next door to a school, complained that he could not work because the children made so much noise.

37. *Analyse and tell parts of speech of words in italics:*

If he had *done what* I told *him*, he would not have been blamed.

38. *Analyse:*

As I walked home, I thought of the pleasant evening I had spent, and I resolved that I would go back again very soon.

39. *Analyse and parse words in italics:*

I did not ask him his *name*, *because* I *knew* what it was.

40. *Analyse:*

Before my friend arrived, I took out my best books so that he might have something to look at.

Write out sentences including these words:

Diffident, deceptive, token, council.

SYNTAX

Rule 1: **A verb must be of the same Person and Number as its Nominative.**

The man sings. I am. She is. We are.

EXERCISE 48

Correct the following:

1. The hills was covered with snow.
2. We was in the garden at the time.

3. Some streets is very dark.
4. A man with his dog were at the door.
5. There is five books here, not four.
6. There were a man here asking for you.
7. Was you told to do that?
8. The price of butter and eggs are very high.
9. To help the poor are the duty of all.

Rule 2. **Two or more Singular Nominatives connected by And require a verb in the Plural.**

Example: James and *Mary* often sing together.

EXERCISE 49

Correct the following:
1. The captain and the mate was washed overboard.
2. You and he was in the same class.
3. These men and I am going to the meeting.
4. The man and his wife was taking a walk.

Rule 3: **Two or more Singular Nominatives connected by Or or Nor require a verb in the Singular.**

Note: **If the Nominatives differ in Person, then the verb agrees with the nearest one.**

If one Nominative is Plural, then the verb is Plural.

EXERCISE 50

Correct the following:
1. Either my brother or I has regularly visited him.
2. The King or his courtiers has betrayed the people.
3. Either Robert or William have taken it.
4. Neither the captain nor the crew was saved.
5. Either George or the gardener have pulled the flowers.

Note: Each, every, either, neither, everyone, everybody, nobody, no one, take a singular verb.

Example: Everybody loves a sailor.
No one tells me the truth.

Rule 4: **The verb To Be requires same case after it as it has before it.**

Example: It was *she* who was to blame.

EXERCISE 51

Correct the following:
1. It was him you saw at the window.
2. You knew quite well it was me.
3. Whether was it her or her sister who sang?
4. If I were him I would not reply.
5. I believe it was her that caused the trouble.
6. Do you know whom it was broke the jug?

Rule 5: **The Past Participle is used after the Verbs, Have and Be.**

EXERCISE 52

Correct the following:
1. She has tore her new book.
2. He has went away an hour ago.
3. They have did it again.
4. The pipes were froze last week.
5. You should have came sooner.
6. He has drank all the milk.

Rule 6: **Transitive Verbs and Prepositions govern the Objective Case.**

Example: I heard *him*.   They spoke to *her*.

EXERCISE 53

Correct the following:
1. Who did you see?
2. They told the story to him and I.
3. Who do you wish to send?
4. He divided the cake between Tom and I.
5. This is the man who your brother helped.

57

Rule 7: **Two Negatives must not be used to express the same thing.**

Example: 'I do not want no more tea', *should be* 'I do not want any more tea'.

Correct the following:

1. She could not speak no louder.
2. We have never seen none of them since.
3. The hens haven't had no meat to-day.
4. After the accident he couldn't remember nothing.
5. We never saw no food for two days.

Rule 8: **After Than or As a Noun or Pronoun is either Nominative to a verb understood or Objective by a verb or preposition understood.**

Example: James is stronger than *I* (am). You helped him more than *me* (than you helped me).

Correct the following:

1. You are bigger than me.
2. They came later than us.
3. The car did not hurt him so much as they.
4. Can she play as well as me?
5. We can do that as well as them.
6. She is smarter than him.
7. They are not as strong as us.

Correct the following:

1. You are a worse speller than me.
2. Neither John nor his sister have seen Paris.
3. Are either of your sisters at home?
4. The two friends are very good to one another.
5. Of the two men my friend is the best player.
6. This is the boy whom I think was to blame.
7. Mr. Smith is the man who have been elected.

8. I would have wrote sooner, if I had not ben so busy.
9. Which of your two sisters is the tallest?
10. We do not like those kind of nuts.
11. We don't want none of your impudence.
12. The money was divided between the four boys.
13. Each of them was served in their turn.
14. He cannot play so well as her.
15. We cannot tell who this book belongs to.
16. Where was you going yesterday?
17. The soldier he told me a wonderful story.
18. We done some work for that firm.
19. We escaped because they never seen us.
20. They have began building some houses there.

WORD-BUILDING

A word in its simplest form is called a ROOT or PRIMARY WORD, as black, board, saw, dust, bed, room.

Now, if we combine two of those Primary words we get a COMPOUND word, *blackboard, sawdust, bedroom.*

EXERCISE 57

(a) *Form Compound Nouns from the following words:*

House, wives, foot, ball, table, cloth, life, belt, door, tomb, out, boot, black, stone, gentle, grand, man, mother, father, water, maid, shed, song, school, servant, bird, master, milk, motor, pick, tooth, cart, cup, pot, tea, egg, light, post, sky, lamp, yard, time, church, piece, car.

(b) *Make sentences using these Compounds.*
Give some additional examples.

Adjectives may be formed by combining two words.

Example: Lion-hearted, everlasting.

EXERCISE 58

Form Compound Adjectives from the following words:

Head, world, in, strong, wide, land, hot, lasting, purse, white, ever, proud, making, health, money, skill, giving, fashioned, full, blue, right, red, spectacled, well, up, ill, old, deserved, hill.

Make sentences using these Compounds.
Give some additional examples.

EXERCISE 59

Form Compound Verbs from the following words:

Take, full, flow, over, fill, wit, out, draw, strip, hold, under, with, bid, say, up, mine, for, gain, run, wash, safe, white, guard, stand.

Make sentences using these Compounds.
Give some additional examples.

FORMATION OF NOUNS, ADJECTIVES AND VERBS FROM EACH OTHER

Words are formed from each other in three ways:

1. By a CHANGE IN THE WORD itself, as grieve, grief.
2. By a PREFIX, as come, *in*come.
3. By a SUFFIX, as wise, wis*dom*.

Note: Prefix is a syllable placed **before** a word.
Suffix is a syllable placed **after** a word.

NOUNS FORMED FROM NOUNS

1. By a change in the word.

NOUN	NOUN	NOUN	NOUN
arc	arch	dale	dell
bank	bench		

2. By a Prefix.

cycle	bi-cycle	rest	un-rest
justice	in-justice	noon	after-noon

3. By a Suffix.

physic	physic-ian	peasant	peasant-ry
hero	hero-ism	pilgrim	pilgrim-age

EXERCISE 60

(a) *Form Nouns from the following Nouns:*
Day, eagle, farm, infant, slave, engine, drug, friend, coat, sense, stream, king, coal, surgeon, workman, knight, neighbour, music, cash, bank, patriot, refuge, ice, part, flower, shade.

(b) *Make sentences containing (i) the root word, (ii) the derivative.*

NOUNS FORMED FROM ADJECTIVES

By a Suffix.

ADJECTIVE	NOUN	ADJECTIVE	NOUN
apt	aptitude	content	content-ment
absent	absent-ee	merry	mirth, (merriment)
wise	wisdom	sincere	sincerity
obedient	obedience	decent	decency

EXERCISE 61

(a) *Form Nouns from the following Adjectives:*

Strong, secure, vacant, young, happy, rude, kind, transparent, royal, warm, feeble, wide, free, true, private, deep, brilliant, long, just, innocent, hard, rapid, weak.

(b) *Make sentences containing (i) root word, (ii) the derivative.*

NOUNS FORMED FROM VERBS

1. By a Change in the word.

VERB	NOUN	VERB	NOUN
advise	advice	sell	sale
choose	choice	feed	food

2. By a Prefix.

cry	out-cry	look	out-look
fit	mis-fit	set	on-set

3. By a Suffix.

school	schol-ar	govern	govern-or
extend	exten-sion	please	pleasure
spin	spin-ster	move	movement

EXERCISE 62

(a) *Form Nouns from the following Verbs:*

Feed, sail, explain, judge, excel, repent, study, attend, preside, serve, abound, amuse, depart, agree, rebel, conquer, manage, beg, occupy, oppress, invent, inspect, create, prove, move, let, sing, come, act.

(b) *Make sentences containing (i) root word, (ii) the derivative.*

ADJECTIVES FORMED FROM NOUNS

1. **By a Change in the word.**

NOUN	ADJECTIVE	NOUN	ADJECTIVE
heat	hot	pride	proud

2. **By a Prefix.**

door	out-door

3. **By a Suffix.**

autumn	autumn-al	gold	gold-en
voice	voice-less	wealth	wealthy
peril	peril-ous	skill	skil-ful

EXERCISE 63

(a) *Form Adjectives from the following Nouns:*

Home, victory, joy, mountain, Kenya, people, anxiety, glory, fool, horror, ocean, guilt. toil, affection, courage, single, circle, splendour, majesty, honour, wool, poet, health, war, fate, leather, nation, voice.

(b) *Make sentences containing (i) root word, (ii) the derivative.*

ADJECTIVES FORMED FROM ADJECTIVES

1. **By a Prefix.**

ADJECTIVE	ADJECTIVE	ADJECTIVE	ADJECTIVE
happy	un-happy	secure	in-secure
agreeable	dis-agreeable	responsible	ir-responsible

2. **By a Suffix.**

many	mani-fold	blithe	blithe-some

EXERCISE 64

(a) *Make Adjectives from the following Adjectives:*

Capable, legal, glad, ripe, blue, wise, honest, pure, regular, possible, noble, true, agreeable, proper, holy, fair, safe, passable, religious.

(b) *Make sentences containing (i) the root word, (ii) the derivative.*

ADJECTIVES FORMED FROM VERBS.

By a Suffix.

VERB	ADJECTIVE	VERB	ADJECTIVE
forget	forget-ful	tire	tire-some

(a) Form Adjectives from following Verbs:
Read, allow, eat, move, tire, meddle, forget, elect.

(b) Make sentences containing (i) the root word, (ii) the derivative.

VERBS FORMED FROM NOUNS

1. By a Change in the word.

NOUN	VERB	NOUN	VERB
glass	glaze	drop	drip
cloth	clothe	knot	knit

2. By a Prefix.

roll	en-roll	friend	be-friend

3. By a Suffix.

length	length-en	magnet	magnet-ise

EXERCISE 66

(a) Form Verbs from the following Nouns:
Thief, grass, frost, life, gold, knee, game, roll, head, blood, knot, strength, danger, camp, prison.

(b) Make sentences containing (i) the root word, (ii) the derivative.

VERBS FORMED FROM ADJECTIVES

1. By a Change in the word.

ADJECTIVE	VERB	ADJECTIVE	VERB
full	fill	hale	heal

2. By a Prefix.

fine	re-fine	able	en-able
dim	be-dim	large	en-large

3. By a Suffix.

simple	simplify	clear	clarify
dark	darken	civil	civil-ise

EXERCISE 67

(a) Form Verbs from the following Adjectives:
Pure, light, dark, calm, numb, large, fine, full, clear, fertile, simple, just, rich, dim, feeble.

(b) Make sentences containing (i) the root word, (ii) the derivative.

VERBS FORMED FROM VERBS

1. **By a Change in the word.**

VERB	VERB	VERB	VERB
sit	set	wake	watch

2. **By a Prefix.**

bid	for-bid	spell	mis-spell

3. **By a Suffix.**

beat	batter	shove	shuffle

EXERCISE 68

(a) *Form Verbs from the following Verbs:*
Rise, tie, do, believe, chat, lead, behave, sprinkle, fall.

(b) *Make sentences containing (i) the root word, (ii) the derivative.*

Printed by Martin's The Printers Ltd., Berwick upon Tweed